Usborne
First Magic Painting
Knights and Castles

Dip the brush into water, then sweep it across each picture to see the paint magically appear.

Use the flap at the back of the book to stop the paint from seeping through to the next page.

Written by Abigail Wheatley
Designed and illustrated by Emily Ritson

Dragons like me aren't scary!

A watery moat surrounds this castle.

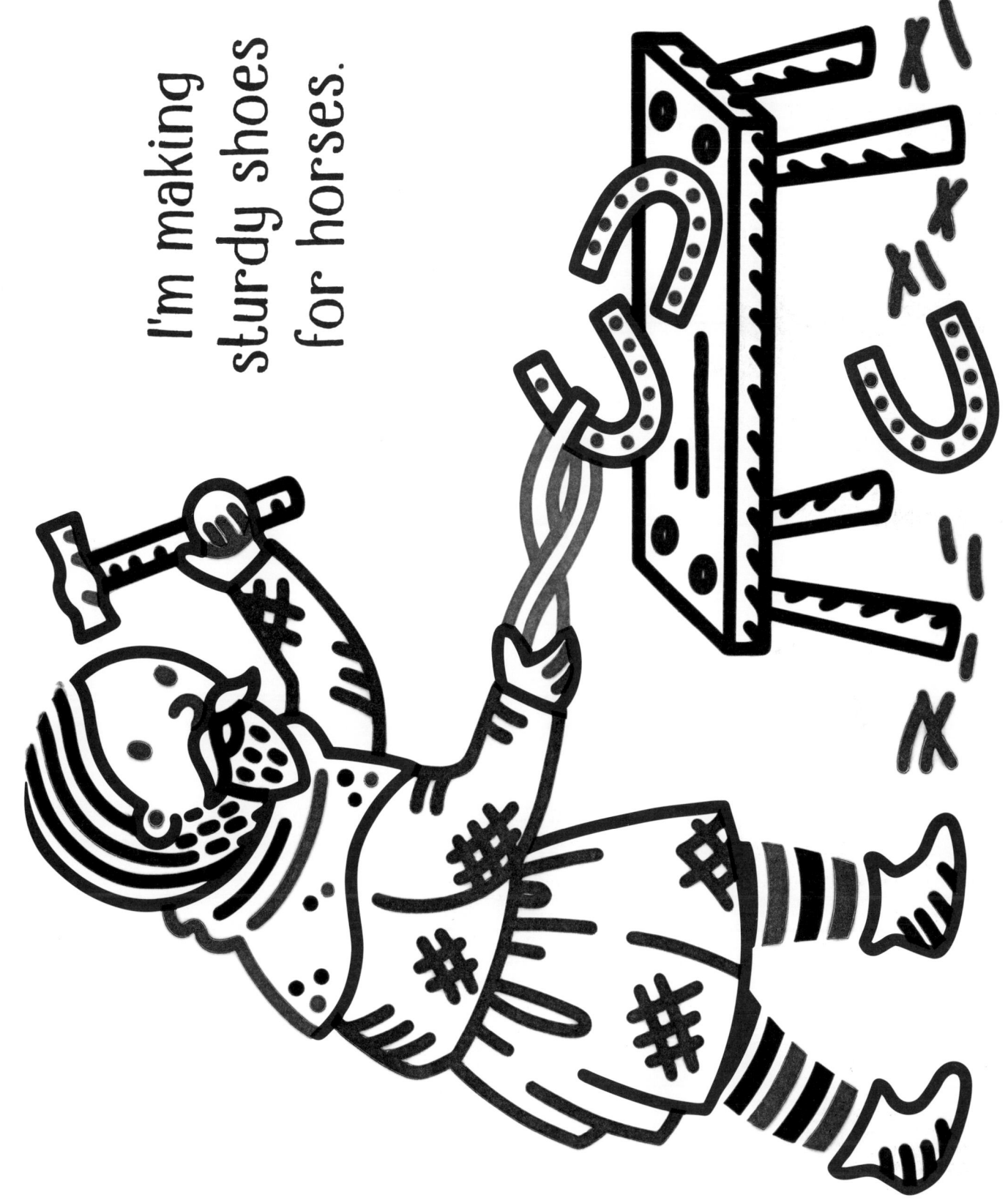

A tall, strong tower

We're ready for an adventure!

I hope I'll be a knight one day...